Don't worry about tomorrow

Matthew 6 v 25-34

because

god's love is as sure as the sunrise

Lamentations 3v22-23

god has good plans for you

Jeremiah 29 v 11

your
future is
safe in
His
hands

Psalm 31 v 14-15

Know that...

God cares for you

you are Precious to Him

1 Peter 5v7 and Isaiah 43v4

He is always with you

Isaiah 43 v 2

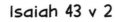

so do
not be
afraid

Joshua 1 v 9

remember

God is faithful to all of His promises

Hebrews 10 v 23

and
nothing
can
separate
you from
His
love

Romans 8 v 39